BREAKING THE CYCLE

BREAKING THE CYCLE

JIM STEPHENS

QuantumQuill Press

CONTENTS

CHAPTER 1

Introduction

Breaking the Cycle: Healing from Toxic Relationships is a book about women who are stuck in a pattern of choosing abusive and controlling men to be in relationships with. This book provides an understanding of why it is these types of women become infatuated with the selfish and unkind men. The book supplies info into the early childhood of the women and how they were raised. The book criticizes the women for being drawn to what the author calls a lover/marshmallow man. This critiquing encourages women to make the effort to change the patterns that have led them into numerous failed relationships with the same type of men. Dr. Harley emphasizes that the only way to make this change is to ask God for the courage, strength, and wisdom to guide them to make the change possible. The author does make it clear that it would be best for these women to stay away from serious relationships with men. Finally, the book gives a step-by-step guide that provides a way that will lead these women to effectively change the patterns of men they choose, to raising self-worth, and finally leading to a healthy relationship. This essay will provide a detailed summary and critique of this book.

CHAPTER 2

Recognizing Toxic Relationships

2.1 Signs of a Toxic Relationship There are numerous signs of a toxic relationship, but some are less obvious than others. These vary in amount and severity depending on the person and situation. All toxic relationships include deceptive control. This control can be financial, pushing you to alter your ways of behavior and thinking, controlling who you interact with and how often. There may be displays of anger and hostility when this is challenged. Another form of control is emotional, where you are blamed for their behavior, shamed, degraded, made to feel guilty, or responsible for their emotional well-being. This is often accompanied by threats to end the relationship, self-harm, or suicide. The control can also be isolating you from your friends and family and having too much say in your personal matters. This all leads to the victim feeling helpless and powerless.

Recognizing that you are in a toxic relationship can be a difficult and painful process. As human beings, we have an incredible ability to see the potential for goodness in others. This can trick us into overlooking the destructive behaviors due to trauma bonding, so that we can see the person our partners could become – not the people they actually are at the present time. Many people are aware that they are in psycho emotionally abusive relationships but cannot identify the patterns within the relationship. This is due to many factors, such as gaslighting, not knowing what a healthy relationship looks like, having been brought up in a dysfunctional family, or experiencing such relationships in their early adult life with peers.

CHAPTER 3

Understanding the Cycle of Toxicity

What complicates matters is that some abusers are quite nice and caring at times. Sociable and likable outside the home, they can be models of good behavior at gatherings with friends or business associates. This Jekyll and Hyde aspect often takes others by surprise. It is also confusing to the person being abused, who sees only the Dr. Jekyll side and asks 'why can't he be like that all the time.' This dual personality is a major reason why the cycle is so difficult to break.

At this point, she will feel the need to 'stand by her man' and help him through his problems. The abuser will then become more abusive and the woman will be in a constant state of fight or flight because of the unpredictability of his actions. She will feel the need to fix him in order to return things to the way they were before. By making her feel responsible for his emotional state and behavior, he can manipulate her into doing whatever he wants. This is when the cycle has become fully fledged.

Understanding how a cycle of toxicity begins and escalates in a relationship is the first step toward breaking free. Initially, the abuser will be attentive and charming. He will make the woman feel that she is the most important person in his life. She will be completely taken in by this and think that she has found her soulmate. Then, the abuser will start to become emotionally abusive and the woman will feel as if he truly does not mean the hurtful things he says.

CHAPTER 4

The Impact of Toxic Relationships on Mental Health

The chapter begins with a study where it is constantly reported that those who engage in romantic relationships with high levels of conflict experience low self-esteem and are generally dissatisfied with life. As discussed in Chapter 2, self-esteem is one of the core self-evaluations and is a key component of our mental health. Those with high self-esteem generally have a positive outlook - considering themselves in a positive light and are usually satisfied with themselves and their relationships. Those with low self-esteem often have a negative outlook and are dissatisfied with themselves and their relationships. It is the negative perception of self that is greatly influenced in toxic relationships, thus resulting in a further reduction of self-esteem. This is particularly noticed when people reflect on the person they were before entering the toxic relationship and can then see the contrast in their personality and the way in which they think about themselves. In doing so, one may develop depressive symptoms. found that individuals' self-esteem can be eroded by negative perceptions from their partners. From such a study, it is seen how in toxic relationships, where emotions are highly negative and volatile, an individual's perception of self can be attacked to an extent where all that remains is negative self-worth. This can be seen as the final straw in the breakdown of mental health as it is self-esteem levels which commonly separate those with good mental health and those with mental health complications such as anxiety and depression.

CHAPTER 5

Breaking Free: Steps to Healing

That being said, there are a number of elements that are relatively consistent in how to break free and heal from a toxic relationship. When someone has a broken leg, the doctor can give a basic timeline on how long it will take to heal, how much therapy is needed, and the vast majority of broken legs will heal on that timeline. Therapy and healing from a toxic relationship is a bit different. The person needs to be truly fed up with things being the way that they are and fully committed to change. Usually, the severity of the relationship will dictate how much therapy is needed, but recovering from codependency and healing fully can be done in less time than you think if you fully commit to recovery measures.

Healing from a toxic relationship is a process much like recovery from an addiction. You will experience denial, anger, confusion, and depression, but unlike dealing with an addiction, the person you miss or think you miss never existed. Codependency treatment is most likely the most difficult as well as the most complicated thing you will ever attempt. You will be fighting with emotions that you believe to be real, but are actually the results of extensive manipulation. A professional therapist who is experienced in the areas of codependency and toxic relationships is your best bet to fully recover.

CHAPTER 6

Setting Boundaries for Healthy Relationships

When you have overcome dependency, when you have begun to respect yourself, you are ready to set boundaries in order to preserve and protect your newly-found self-respect. This may be intimidating, especially if you have not had a positive role model for setting boundaries. You may feel guilty, selfish, or disloyal. You may have anxiety and fear retribution. You may be so used to others violating your boundaries that you are not even sure what they are. There are a few simple steps to setting boundaries. First, you need to know yourself and identify what is right for you. This might take some quiet time alone. If you are not used to thinking about what you want, this may be a difficult task for you. After you have identified your needs, you need to respect them. This means saying "no" to a request that you would rather not do and not feeling guilty afterwards. Respecting your boundaries also involves taking action if someone violates your limits. This might involve taking a stand on the spot or removing yourself from the situation and the relationship. Boundary setting is a skill and it will take time and practice to get it right. But it can be done, and it is worth it. You will find that people will have increased respect for you, and you will feel a greater sense of self-respect. Setting these limits is another way of living in the solution, taking responsibility for yourself, and respecting others' right to do the same. As assertive behavior becomes a part of your life, you will find that you have fewer conflicts, and that other people are not able to manipulate you so easily.

CHAPTER 7

Building Self-Esteem and Confidence

The next step is to take your new beliefs about yourself and put them into action by doing things that will help to raise your self-esteem. This can be achieved in a number of ways and will be covered in further detail. For now, look at the list you made in Tuning in to Yourself about the things you used to enjoy doing. It's likely that you didn't pursue these things while in your toxic relationship, or that you were made to feel bad about doing them. Promise yourself that you will try to do these things again or try new things. Start off with something small and work your way up. You may feel anxious about doing things without your partner or guilty for having fun, but tell yourself that it's OK and you deserve it. Remember that it's all part of the process of change. Take your time with these steps, and remember that it's OK to take breaks and come back to them at a later date. Changes in the way you feel about yourself won't happen overnight; they're a work in progress.

Once you begin to see that some of your beliefs about yourself are unfounded, you can make the decision to let go of them and leave them in the past where they belong. It can be useful to write them down and then write a list of alternative positive beliefs about yourself. For example, change "I'm a useless parent" to "I'm a good enough parent, and no one is perfect, everyone makes mistakes. I can learn from mine."

Repeat these new beliefs and visualize them in your mind. Consider them to be your new mantra, and if you find yourself slipping back to your old beliefs, stop and remind yourself of the new belief. It won't be easy at first, and you may not believe what you're saying, but keep at it and you will begin to notice a shift in your way of thinking and feeling about yourself.

The first step in building your self-esteem and confidence is to challenge and change the negative beliefs you hold about yourself. If you were involved with a toxic partner, chances are you've been told that you're worthless, a bad parent, ugly, stupid, and that no one else would want you. You may also have been told that you'd never amount to anything. It's important to challenge these beliefs by asking yourself where they originated from. Was it from your partner, or someone else from earlier in your life? It's likely that you may have developed these beliefs about yourself during your childhood, whether through family, friends, teachers, or other influential people. Ask yourself if there is any hard evidence to support these beliefs, and try to identify evidence that doesn't support them. It can be helpful to get a new perspective by asking a friend whether they would have the same opinion of you if they knew the same things that you've done. You may be surprised by how much the other person thinks.

CHAPTER 8

Seeking Professional Help and Support

Professional support can be invaluable in the healing process. A qualified therapist can help you make sense of your experiences and feelings, and help you work through complex emotions. A therapist can also help you identify attitudes and beliefs that may be holding you back from experiencing more satisfying relationships in the future. Choose a therapist who is experienced in working with survivors of abusive relationships, and make sure that the therapist is willing to let you set the pace for your healing process. There should be a good rapport between you and your therapist. You should feel that the therapist understands the issues and is on your side. If you feel uneasy with the therapist, it is alright to find another one. Helplines and support groups can also be a valuable source of assistance. It can be a great relief to talk to people who understand what you are going through. This can also be a good way to make supportive friends. Listening to others' experiences and being able to help and support others are also good ways to help yourself.

CHAPTER 9

Letting Go of Guilt and Shame

When we leave a toxic relationship, it is not unusual to feel guilty. We may feel we have let the other person down or that if we had tried harder, we could have helped them. We may feel we have failed. We may also feel guilt and shame about the part we played in allowing the toxic relationship to develop, about ignoring those initial warning signs, about not maintaining our boundaries, and about allowing someone to treat us and talk to us in ways that are unacceptable. These feelings are completely normal, but they are not rational. The phenomenon of guilt and shame is often deep-seated and is an inappropriate and unhealthy form of self-reproach. If you feel guilt and shame perpetually and find it impossible to shake, there may be an unresolved issue from the past influencing your feelings. Therapy can help you release yourself from such damaging emotions and address any underlying issues that have influenced your experiences in toxic relationships.

CHAPTER 10

Forgiveness: A Path to Healing

Work can be very useful in overcoming feelings of powerlessness from the past. Perhaps you can become an advocate for survivors of abuse or volunteer in a self-help group. It is vital to stop any self-blame by understanding that it is never the survivor's fault and remember that personal boundaries are everyone's right. Take good care of yourself in the healing process. This is also a time when it is appropriate to think about forgiveness, but do not rush yourself. It is a common belief that forgiveness is necessary or even that it is for the benefit of the perpetrator. However, it is not so much an act for them but a gift to yourself. At a time when you feel your abuser no longer has any emotional hold on you, you can consider trying a Forgiveness Letter to complete the healing process. An example of this letter can be found at the end of this article.

Anger often replaces grief in the healing process. Letting go of rage is a goal in recovery from toxic relationships. This process involves fully feeling the anger in order to totally resolve it. An effective way to do this is to sit alone and write a letter to the abuser. It can be useful to write down all the things you wish you could say to them, tell them how they have hurt you and express your rage to its full extent. Then when it's all out on paper, you burn the letter and with it let go of the anger. At this stage, it is also important to look at any resentments you may hold against people who did not protect you or take your side.

CHAPTER 11

Cultivating Self-Care Practices

Self-care is a vital aspect of your recovery because it helps you to reintegrate your life purpose and passions and establish high self-esteem. Coming out of a toxic relationship may have been quite a shock from constantly striving to please your partner and getting highly self-critical to avoid criticism. Low self-esteem and self-neglect might have reached an all-time high, causing you to give up hobbies and things that you used to do for fun. By taking care of yourself and rediscovering forgotten joys, you're re-establishing your self-identity which is crucial to healing. High self-esteem also provides you with the strength and resilience to cope with life's more difficult and unexpected moments. By showing yourself that you are worthy of love and comfort, you won't fall back into the self-neglect that's accompanied by the numbing down of harmful coping mechanisms.

Developing a self-care routine is beneficial for recovering from any kind of trauma, and toxic relationships can be very traumatizing. At the basis, self-care is very simple and straightforward: it's anything that you do to take care of yourself. We want to focus on cultivating comforting and simple self-care routines to help you destress and manage anxiety. Instead of turning to harmful coping mechanisms such as binge-eating, drugs, or excessive drinking, self-care can serve as a positive alternative.

If you've been in an unhealthy relationship for a while, you may have forgotten what it's like to do things that make you happy.

CHAPTER 12

Rebuilding Trust in Relationships

While trusting oneself and one's judgments, it is important to implement a support system based upon encouraging and reliable individuals. This is a definite improvement from the support you may have had in past toxic relationships. Opening up and sharing past experiences and feelings with a close friend or therapist may lead to helpful feedback and alternative perspectives regarding the relationships which you are healing from. Take your time in re-establishing a sense of trust in others. Do not rush into relationships or conversations that you do not feel comfortable with. At this point, it is crucial to be in tune with your feelings and instincts surrounding others. If something does not feel right, it probably isn't. This intuition is often stronger than its given credit for. In essence, healthy relationships are based upon equality, respect and understanding. This is the precedent for the relationship you should attempt to gauge with others.

Securing one's progress in healing from toxic relationships typically involves reclaiming a sense of trust in others and oneself. You will have to understand, however, that you are a proficient judge of character, as evidenced by your completion of unhealthy relationships. Learning to rebuild trust can simultaneously occur in the formation of healthy relationships and in the evolution of the relationship you have with yourself.

CHAPTER 13

Nurturing Healthy Connections

By now, we have likely been experiencing the ending of many unhealthy relationships. We need not feel bad about this because what is happening is making room for healthy connections to manifest. It is better to be alone than to be with those who do not hold our best interests at heart. We must have total trust and a strong feeling of peace with people to call these relationships healthy. They will be supportive and encouraging of us and who we want to be in life. These connections are established through clear communication because one of the major aspects of a healthy relationship is mirrored understanding between both parties. We must be clear about what we want and delicately ensure that those we are involving ourselves with are willing to provide that. Clarity and intuition play a large role in the establishment of healthy connections.

When we've taken the time to establish a strong foundation in our relationship with ourselves and have continued to grow in our practice with maintaining healthy boundaries, the task of creating healthy connections with others becomes a matter of simply remaining aware to ensure that we are (or are continuously working to) expressing our truth and the resolve to never settle for less than we deserve. This sounds relatively easy, especially in comparison to the rest of the work we've done to this point, but maintaining and nurturing healthy connections with others is an ongoing process that requires continuous awareness and commitment.

CHAPTER 14

Creating a Supportive Network

The final step to healing from unhealthy relationships is to get the support you need to stay on the path that leads away from hurt and towards healthy connections with others. Healing from toxic relationships is a long and often painful journey. To help someone stay on the path, the support of friends, family, and therapists is crucial. Without this help, one may be likely to retreat to the familiar pattern of seeking solace in relationships that feel safe—those that recreate past experiences of being taken care of by someone who is also emotionally unhealthy. The initial tendencies to be disbelieving, self-punishing, and/or reliving the abusive experiences can be overwhelming. At times this phase of a survivor's recovery creates concerns for friends and family that may lead to decreased support. It is at these times that a survivor needs to make a special effort to connect with those who understand the recovery process, can validate the survivor's experiences without promoting retribution, and can offer hope of the survivor finding a position of strength. At this point, it is important to connect with a therapist who understands the impact of trauma from the abuser with whom the survivor has had a mixed experience of love and pain. Co-counseling, in which participants take turns being the client and the counselor, with another survivor can be a powerful and cost-effective way of gaining support with the additional benefit of increased understanding of one's experience through helping someone else.

CHAPTER 15

Overcoming Fear of Vulnerability

Remember that intimate settings can produce anxiety because of the perceived need to live up to partners' exalted expectations. A person might feel unworthy of someone else's love and fearful that expectations for him or her will be too high. These fears can lead to feeling uncomfortable in sharing heartaches and weaknesses. It is sometimes believed that there isn't room for mistakes in relationships. People forget that with every learning process, mistakes are made. It is important when entering new relationships to constantly remind ourselves that it is ok to be human and humans are not infallible. This requires giving ourselves and our partners a margin for error, and more room to express feelings and worries. A person must also realize that no matter how independent he or she is, it is ok to depend on someone else to uplift them in times of hardship. With patience and a trusting heart, fears of vulnerability can be overcome.

CHAPTER 16

Redefining Love and Relationships

Traditional male/female roles are not always helpful, nor are they based upon the balanced sharing of energies between two people. This topic is worthy of exploration in itself, the deciding factor in whether a relationship will further one's spiritual growth, or hinder it. Step parenting adds another dimension and set of difficulties to relationships and family dynamics which must be taken into consideration.

A foundation must be laid, one which allows open communication and gives each partner a feeling of safety and trust. Relationship building and bonding is often compared to the construction of a house.

The basic principles for successful relationships are dependent upon similar factors to those that lead to healing. A conscious effort to dedicate oneself to a change in pattern, becoming aware of internal wounds and needs, is necessary to avoid slipping into old ways. Essential here is the support and knowing involvement of another or others.

Once the toxic relationship is a thing of the past and the pieces have been picked up, many seekers find themselves preoccupied with the notion of future love. The idea of trusting another soul with one's sacred heart can be daunting, but view the following teaching as a chance to learn to walk again where the path is now cleared of wreckage.

CHAPTER 17

Embracing Personal Growth and Development

Change is the only evidence of life, and growth is its most intimate mode of change. If we try to inhibit growth or any kind of change, we are trying to inhibit life. This can be for many reasons, but for survivors of toxic relationships, the reason is probably because change has been forced upon them before they were ready and/or in a form that was unwanted. A key point to remember is that by realizing that you have survived a relationship, you recognize that some part of you is not broken beyond repair. Fundamentally, some sense of self has survived and is likely a positive starting point to begin building a new life. This is a restoration of hope and your most vital tool in growth - hope that things can be different from the pain that has been endured. By using that hope as a foundation, survivors can begin to start building new lives for themselves, deciding upon the sort of life that they would like to lead, and then taking steps to achieve it. Becoming goal-directed can be important, especially for those who have been stuck in purely reactive roles for a long time. It is important to recognize that you have the ability to enact change in your life and then plug into that sense of control. Deciding on a broad direction can be enough. Remember, it takes considerable practice to disconnect from negative past experiences, and learning to constructively reflect on failures/mistakes is a part of the healing process, not a separate failure in itself. High expectations in early learning stages can often lead to relapse into negative self-blame patterns. Step back and keep moving forward.

CHAPTER 18

Learning from Past Mistakes

Never disregard the message that something from your past was good. The thing that was good was the lesson. Remember what the lesson was. Write down the most important lesson you have learned from the experience. Always be looking for red flags. Use the 3 strike rule. This is all about how you perceive people when getting to know them. Everyone has good and bad points. Three points of bad will easily tilt the scales in the wrong direction. Red flags alert you to where the bad points are usually found. They should never be ignored or justified. Write them down, give it a strike and date it. If the same person has three strikes for different things, get rid of them. This is all about giving people a chance, whilst not settling for lower than you deserve. Have enough respect for yourself to be willing to let go of anyone that disrespects you. Your time and energy are precious, don't waste it on others. Know when to walk away.

CHAPTER 19

Recognizing and Addressing Codependency

Codependent behavior is learned by watching and imitating other family members who display this type of behavior, and it is an emotional survival strategy. Because codependency is learned, it can also be unlearned. In order to change, it is important that codependents learn to identify their feelings and needs and then begin to assertively meet them in healthy ways. Codependents generally do not know they have feelings and needs. They are so used to focusing on the needs of others and/or controlling a certain situation that they often are unaware of their own motivations. By unearthing hidden feelings and confusions and beginning to gain a real self, a codependent can begin to work through these issues. Using some of the techniques outlined in the rest of the workbook, a codependent can start learning new ways of relating to others and begin to break the cycle by addressing the toxic bonds in their life.

This section defines codependency as a learned behavior that can be passed down from one generation to another. It is an emotional and behavioral condition that affects an individual's ability to have a healthy, mutually satisfying relationship. It is also known as "relationship addiction" because people with codependency often form or maintain relationships that are one-sided, emotionally destructive, and/or abusive.

This section outlines how to recognize codependency within yourself and then how to begin addressing it.

CHAPTER 20

Healing Childhood Trauma

Understanding the impact of childhood trauma on the quality of our lives is the first step to making changes. Many trauma survivors may feel "stuck" or feel that they are always in "crisis mode." The chaos and trauma they experienced growing up become the "norm" in their lives and they may not know any other way of living. When things are going well, they may fear that the other shoe will drop. They may have a history of self-sabotaging and making decisions that are not in their best interest. All of these are signs that childhood trauma has had a lasting impact on their lives. Next, we must consider seeking therapy. Therapy is an important tool for survivors of trauma. With the help of a therapist, survivors can work through their past and the impact it has had on their lives. With therapy, survivors can also work on issues of self-worth and begin to make positive changes in their lives. Finally, survivors must be patient with themselves and practice self-care in their healing process. Changing a lifetime of patterns is not easy, and setbacks are part of the process.

Childhood trauma can set the stage for a pattern of bad relationships throughout adult life. Childhood trauma can be obvious, such as physical abuse, sexual abuse, or neglect. It can also be less obvious, emotional abuse or witnessing a dysfunctional relationship between our parents.

Many adults who have experienced traumatic events as children are not aware of the lasting impact left on them. They may feel that the past is unchangeable and resign themselves to thinking "I turned out ok". It is important that survivors of adverse childhood experiences understand that the past does not have to dictate their future. With hard work, healing, and support, it is possible to change patterns and make better choices in our adult lives.

Healing from toxic relationships means that we figure out how to break the cycle of unhealthy relationship patterns and to avoid toxic partners in the future. One of the most important things in healing from toxic relationships involves understanding and healing childhood trauma. Our childhood and early experiences have a tremendous impact on the choices we make as adults. If we grew up with chaos, we may be drawn to chaotic or unpredictable situations. If we were taught that we are not worthy of love, we may settle for being treated poorly.

CHAPTER 21

Practicing Mindfulness
and Meditation

Meditation is often easier said than done, and many people have difficulty with it at first. We sit quietly, with a focused attention on an object such as the breath. When the mind wanders, we notice it and bring it back to the attention. Meditation brings a deeper level of relaxation to the mind and body and offers many emotional and physical healing benefits. Mindfulness and meditation together can release the chronic tension, depression, and anxiety that is so developed from trauma and abusive experiences. These practices teach us acceptance of the present, change our cognitive awareness, and dissolve our tendencies to avoid and escape reality. Through finding peace within ourselves, we can let go of resentments and find forgiveness for those who have hurt us.

One of the most difficult, yet rewarding parts of the healing process is finding inner peace. We seek peace from the constant negative thoughts placed upon us from our abusers, and gain a higher self-worth to know we are worthy of love and respect. Through the consistent practice of mindfulness and meditation, we can learn to quiet our mind and let go of the thoughts and worries that keep us stuck in the past. Mindfulness is the practice of paying attention to the present experience with an open and accepting mindset. It is more than just taking a break from negative thoughts, but changing the way we relate to these thoughts.

With enough practice, we can become an observer of these thoughts. We can let them flow in and out of our minds without getting caught up in the high emotional reactions they bring and the stories behind them. An exercise to practice mindfulness to thought is sitting comfortably, closing the eyes, and paying attention to the breath. Whenever a thought arises, notice it, and bring attention back to the breath. Over and over, notice and return.

CHAPTER 22

Expressing Emotions in a Healthy Way

Secondary emotions have been defined as emotions that are reactions to other emotions. In the context of shame and guilt, anger and feeling misunderstood or judged might be the former. Hurt and disappointment may be the secondary emotions that develop from other emotions such as sadness or fear. When dealing with these complex emotions, it is important to be insightful and authentic. You must ask yourself what you are really feeling, what caused you to feel this way, and whether your reaction is proportional to the event. Being empathetic to yourself and realizing that it is okay to feel are also important steps in expressing these complex emotions. Write about them in your journal, talk to a friend, draw or paint, or work through it with a therapist. Remember to be patient and persistent because expression of these emotions is not an easy step, it may take time. But it will help to prevent the cycle of unresolved feelings leading to problematic behavior or further emotional difficulty.

CHAPTER 23

Identifying and Challenging Negative Thought Patterns

The first step in challenging negative thoughts lies in identifying the thoughts themselves. Often, a negative thought is so automatic that it goes unnoticed. Therefore, it is important to become aware of these thoughts in order to challenge them. This can be done by recording thoughts in a diary, specific to the situation in which they arose. An individual can then take time to reflect on their thought process, assessing the thoughts for accuracy and their effect on mood. Once negative thoughts have been identified, it is then possible to move to the next stage of challenging them.

Cognitive Behavioural Therapy (CBT) is a very useful framework in addressing negative thought patterns. This therapy is based upon the theory that an individual's thoughts are intrinsically linked to their feelings and behaviours, therefore by challenging unhelpful thoughts, a person can become more positive and effective in their actions. To challenge negative thinking, there are a series of CBT techniques which can be used.

CHAPTER 24

Empowering Yourself through Education and Knowledge

Now you might want to discover the way in which these folks have entered into your life, how you have met them, and more importantly, how the relationship with them began. Usually, a relationship which has begun in an unhealthy way will continue in the same pattern. This info will then give you a clue as to where you'll want to stop any happening similar in the future.

More often than not, if we find that we are continually getting into a similar type of unhealthy/harmful relationship, there's a style and/or emotional behavior there that is causing us to become attracted to a similar kind of person. One method to work out exactly what this specific pattern tends to be is to put in writing all of the attributes and behaviors of the folks that we have had unhealthy relationships with. Then take a look and see if there are any common demographics. For example, work status, age, or interests. If no common demographic is apparent, it's likely that it's a specific behavior type that you are attracted/related to. This is the point it may get tough to face up to some of your own behaviors and acknowledge they could be negative. But considering that you like to be successful in breaking the cycle of toxic relationships, it's very important to be completely honest with yourself.

Trying to find any hidden secret to curing your heartbreak? Wish to discover why it is that you are feeling like you are caught up in that toxic romantic relationship and things don't actually feel any different? Well, you have to pinpoint precisely what the issue is plus where it all started. All of us who've stored making the same exact errors are inclined to do this for an excuse.

CHAPTER 25

Finding Strength in Spirituality

Spirituality is a personal connection to something greater than oneself. It may be tied to concrete religious doctrine and community participation, it may be perceived as a life force or divine essence that exists in all things, or it may be considered an illusion that helps people cope with the stark realities of existence. Empirical research indicates that higher levels of spirituality are conducive to overall better mental health and adaptability to stressful life events. Spirituality is inherently therapeutic. It often involves attempting to rise above the lower human instincts and emotions in order to connect with a higher plane of existence. This is especially relevant to healing from toxic relationships because it is common to feel consumed by anger, hatred, and jealousy. While it is not healthy to repress these emotions, they will be easier to cope with and understand if you simultaneously work to cultivate higher virtues. Some people may already have a strong spiritual life and others may be looking to develop a new or renewed sense of purpose. Wherever you are in this process, consider how you can use your spiritual beliefs to help you understand and transcend the pain of the past.

If you are struggling to build your life back up after a toxic relationship, look within for new strengths and interests that you can now cultivate. Whether you are connected to a religious tradition or not, it is worth considering the power of spirituality as a healing agent. It is helpful to distinguish between religiosity and spirituality. You may practice a formal religion, you may feel spiritual without identifying with a specific institution, you may reject spirituality or religious belief of any kind. Religiosity is the involvement with an organized community of belief. It will benefit you to understand how patterns of religiosity and spirituality affect interpersonal and personal behavior so that you can make explicit decisions on how to incorporate or adapt these activities to the benefit of your new life.

CHAPTER 26

Embracing a Positive Mindset

A good way to integrate it into your subconscious mind is through the use of affirmations (I will explain this later) and looking for and acknowledging any evidence which supports this new belief. For example, 'I helped an old lady across the street, that was a nice thing to do. I am a decent human being'. Over time, this belief will become automatic, you will notice a change in self-image and identity.

Ask yourself, do I want to believe this? Is this belief helping me in my life? If the belief is not helping you and you do not want to believe it, then you have the power to change it. The belief that you are a 'no hoper' can be changed to 'I have the potential to be a great human being'. At first, it will feel very weird and uncomfortable. You will not believe it, you will think that you are deluding yourself. This is the mind looking for consistency in belief and attitude. We do not like to change our beliefs because it will challenge our comfort zones and often our sense of identity. Do not be deterred, with persistence, this belief can be changed.

The first one (like all the others) is only a belief - it is not right, it is not wrong. However, holding this belief will benefit you greatly. In life, you are often told 'you'll never amount to anything'. This is a common belief in many societies. Listen to your own truth, what do you believe?

Do you really believe that you are a 'no hoper', that you will never be a decent human being or fulfill your dreams and aspirations? For many of you, these questions will provoke a feeling of discomfort inside. This is good, this is the first step to change.

- Belief in the potential of all human beings. - Belief that 'I can learn to do anything I want to'.

Learn what these beliefs are - where they come from.

CHAPTER 27

Creating a Life of Purpose and Fulfillment

Packing and selling the stuff didn't really hit me until I started selling off the big ticket items. A dining room set that I only bought a year ago, the red sectional that R and I bought when we moved here to Georgia; it was bittersweet and I felt a mix of sadness and anger while dealing with the furniture. It angered me to let it go for next to nothing, but I kept trying to remind myself that it was just stuff. The anger would be a consistent emotion for me while packing. I was angry for allowing myself to get into this situation. I was angry for being so stupid to think something like this could ever have worked. I haven't let anger consume me and the last time I was consumed with anger I spent four months camping in a bottle of vodka; this time there will be no relapse, there will only be moving forward. It was a good mentality and every day it becomes a stronger reality for me.

CHAPTER 28

Celebrating Progress and Success

Setting small achievable goals and then taking time out to acknowledge and reward ourselves when these are achieved is an important part of the process. This can be as simple as shouting yourself a new book or taking time out to visit a friend. By sharing your goals with a trusted friend or counselor, you are more likely to have the added incentive to see it through, plus you have the benefit of having someone to share your success with. This is a very powerful tool in changing the way we feel about ourselves.

In building self-esteem, it is important to acknowledge that this is a lifelong process and there is no finishing line, rather it is a journey with many triumphs and a fair share of mistakes. Often we are very good at acknowledging our failures and mistakes and dismiss our achievements, or we do not give ourselves permission to take the time to celebrate.

When you have worked through these stages of recognizing abuse, building your self-esteem, and valuing yourself as an important person, you are beginning to create a new life for yourself. You have invested a great deal of time and effort and have taken risks to change. Celebrating your progress and success validates your hard work.

CHAPTER 29

Embracing Healthy Relationships

Unlock the benefits of embracing healthy relationships and learn how they can create an amazing, simple life. Good relationships lead to better health, wellbeing, and a greater chance at a simple life. Get together with your partner and take time to reflect on what you both have seen and discuss what part of the life change process you'd like to be in. Set goals towards a simple life at the start of each week, to suffer and give up an undesirable way of life, by saying things such as "This week we will do X to make life more simple." Take time to educate and encourage your children about the benefits of a simple life by using examples from your own life or other people's lives. Agree that it is something you would like for them in the future. This will promote a positive family team environment and, with everyone in agreement, will make the life change process much smoother and more successful. Living a clear, focused, and clutter-free life will allow more time and energy to be put into your relationships. With less time needed on home maintenance and many of the lessons children will be learning during the life change process, you will have more time and energy to invest in your marriage.

CHAPTER 30

Maintaining Boundaries and Self-Care Practices

Withdrawing from a toxic relationship, you have to be prepared to experience some loneliness because you are so used to relating your self-worth to the opinions of another. This is a great opportunity to practice self-care measures.

Action is taken on another person ignoring your boundary by a process called self-advocacy. This is where you speak to the other person about how you are feeling and why, after assessing the situation and your feelings to make sure you are in the right. You must approach the person in a non-aggressive manner and be open, allowing them to explain their actions in order to come to a compromise or to let the person know that you will not tolerate if the behavior continues. Unfortunately, this does not always work, and you will have to take action in terminating the relationship with the person or reducing your contact with them. This may be hard dismissing someone you care about; however, if they continue to disregard your feelings, they are not treating you as a friend or loved one should. Remember, it is OK to end a relationship that you feel is not working for you. It is not an indication of personal failure, and it may well be the best thing for both of you.

There is a misconception about boundaries that implementing them makes you "selfish". This is simply not true. In order to effectively care for others, you must first take care of yourself and your needs. You must then be able to effectively communicate to others what your boundaries are. People are not mind readers, and it is quite unfair to expect someone to know what you will and will not put up with without you telling them. This in no way guarantees that your boundaries will not be crossed, but the true test is sticking with them and taking the appropriate action when they are crossed. If you do not maintain your boundary, this will give the other person "permission" to ignore it and, more often than not, cause you to feel resentful.

Boundaries are a verbal and nonverbal set of rules of how you will take in treatment from others and what action will be taken if they are crossed. When you have no boundaries, a partner believes that they can behave however they would like and you will put up with it. This is what we were explaining when we said that leaving a toxic relationship without making changes would most likely lead to another toxic relationship.

CHAPTER 31

Spreading Awareness and Helping Others

Survivors who are parents have an additional opportunity to prevent abuse by raising their children very differently than they themselves were raised. Breaking the cycle for our own families can be one of the most rewarding experiences in life. By taking positive parenting courses, reading parenting and child development books, learning nonviolent conflict resolution, and exploring alternatives to corporal punishment, we can gain the skills and knowledge that our own parents lacked. It is vitally important to understand that instinct and the normal ways of parenting will often betray us when our 'normal' is all that we have ever known. At these times, we must be gentle with ourselves and with our children and recognize that learning something new is a process which at times includes mistakes. Changing ourselves and our parenting is hard work, but it can be done, and the effects may be seen within a single generation. By guarding our children well and teaching them to be aware of healthy and unhealthy relationship dynamics, we can break the cycle in our own families.

What the survivor chooses to do varies. There are those who become involved in politics, social policy, and law, working to change society's views and the responses of various systems to domestic violence and child abuse. Others may be called to help in specific areas, for example, going back to school for a career in counseling, psychology, psychiatry, or psychiatric nursing. Some survivors prefer more informal roles, running informal support groups online or in their communities, writing articles on the web or elsewhere, and some find it sufficient to be able to speak out when the occasion arises in their daily lives. Whatever course is chosen, awareness can be raised simply by telling our own stories. We can help to dispel the myth that abuse happens only to a certain 'type' of woman or that abuse occurs in no other families than those which are poor, uneducated, or 'dysfunctional'. We can counter beliefs that abuse is caused by alcohol, drugs, stress, or poor anger management, and that an abuser is basically a good person who is only bad sometimes. We can speak about the ways in which our own situations defied these stereotypes.

The strongest advocates and educators among you will likely find that the best way to heal and come to terms with your own experiences is to spread awareness. There is little purpose in what occurred if we learn nothing from it and neither educate nor help others who may be following in our footsteps. Those who have left an abusive relationship and have reached a fairly secure and peaceful place in their lives have a social responsibility. To do no more in life than enjoy the peace and happiness that has been so hard won is to ignore the suffering of untold others who continue to live out their own private hells. Your understanding of what began in your own childhood and about toxic adult relationships can be used to help others.

CHAPTER 32

Conclusion

The Butterfly Room will remain open an online asset that you simply fair can return to all through your travel, or suggest back to as and after you have got. Wishing you all the simplest as you travel against recuperating and mending from the negative levels of energy of the past and towards a brighter, more joyful and more joyful future.

In any case, we come to understand that the travel towards recovery and mending from poisonous connections may be a individual one, wandered at an alternate pace and separate from others. It is my trust that the thoughts and methodologies conferred in this course can offer assistance and bolster to all who wander it.

Thank you for setting out on this excursion with me. It's been an awe-inspiring and overpowering excursion for numerous individuals through coaching and counselling and moving. Now and then this travel begins with an internal tone which might be a still, unassuming little voice which says "I merit better than this." This travel is regularly attempted for the purpose of children. There are moreover adolescents who have seen the light with respect to their claim encounters in grown-up connections and are on a travel to form beyond any doubt that they don't rehash the cycle.

9 798330 617739